Scott Foresman

Math Around the Clock

SUMMER SCHOOL · AFTER SCHOOL · INTERSESSION

Algebra: Expressions and Equations

PEARSON
Scott Foresman

Editorial Offices:
Glenview, Illinois • Parsippany, New Jersey • New York, New York

Sales Offices:
Parsippany, New Jersey • Duluth, Georgia • Glenview, Illinois
Coppell, Texas • Ontario, California • Mesa, Arizona

ISBN: 0-328-06371-1

Copyright © 2003 Pearson Education, Inc.

2 3 4 5 6 7 8 9 10 V004 12 11 10 09 08 07 06 05 04 03

Math Around the Clock

Contents

Unit 6 • Algebra: Expressions and Equations

Each week, Mrs. Cox has her groceries delivered to her home. She pays $5 for delivery, plus the cost of the groceries. Complete the table to find how much she spends each week.

Cost of Groceries	n	$58	$36	$45	$39
Total Cost	$n + 5$				

Expressions with Addition and Subtraction   **LESSON PRACTICE**

Example 1

Find the value of $n + 9$ when $n = 12$.

Substitute 12 for n. Then add.

$n + 9 = 21$
$\downarrow$
$12 + 9 = 21$

Example 2

Find the missing number in the table.

Substitute 46 for x in the expression $x - 5$.

$x - 5$
$\downarrow$
$46 - 5 = 41$

The missing number is 41.

x	$x - 5$
7	2
15	10
23	18
46	

Evaluate each expression for $b = 6$.

1 $b - 4$ _____

2 $3 + b$ _____

3 $8 - b$ _____

4 $13 + b - 1$ _____

Evaluate each expression for $c = 11$.

5 $c + 10$ _____

6 $14 - 5 + c$ _____

7 $11 - c$ _____

8 $15 - c$ _____

9 Evaluate $\triangle - 30$ for $\triangle = 55$. _____

10 Evaluate $6 - \blacksquare$ for $\blacksquare = 3$. _____

© Scott Foresman

5

Name _____

Expressions with Addition and Subtraction (continued)

Evaluate each expression for $m = 18$.

11 $m - 6$ **12** $20 - m$ **13** $5 + m - 14$ **14** $50 - m$

_____   _____   _____   _____

Evaluate each expression for $t = 5$.

15 $8 - t$ **16** $12 + t$ **17** $t + 6 - 10$ **18** $14 - t$

_____   _____   _____   _____

Complete each table.

19

x	$x - 4$
4	0
9	5
15	
	17

20

a	$30 - a$
	27
10	20
18	
30	0

21

n	$7 + n$
6	
15	22
20	27
50	

22

z	$12 - z$
0	12
5	
7	5
10	

23 Evaluate ▲ $- 21$ for ▲ $= 35$. _____

24 Jeff is three years younger than Steve. Complete the table to show Jeff's age.

Steve's age	n	10	15	21	35
Jeff's age	$n - 3$				

25 **Test Prep** Choose the correct letter for the answer.

What is the value of $m + 7$ when $m = 14$?

A 21   **B** 7   **C** 20   **D** 22

1 What is the value of $d - 6$ when $d = 13$?

A 6

B 7

C 8

D 9

2 Evaluate ▲ + 21 for ▲ = 11.

F 10

G 21

H 30

J 32

3 Which of the numbers completes the table?

m	$m - 9$
12	3
19	10
25	16
36	

A 25   C 29

B 27   D 30

4 What is the value of $50 - x$ when $x = 12$?

F 38

G 48

H 28

J 18

5 Which of the numbers completes the table?

c	$15 + c$
0	15
5	20
13	28
27	

A 27   C 42

B 32   D 52

6 Evaluate 64 − ■ for ■ = 22.

F 22

G 26

H 32

J 42

Oral Directions Choose the correct letter for each answer.

Think about this number sentence: 4 + 1 = 2 + 3. Using each of the same digits once, form a new number sentence that uses subtraction.

Name _____

Equations

Example

Solve the equation $x - 6 = 5$ by testing values for x.

Try	$x - 6 = 5$	Does $x - 6 = 5$?
$x = 6$	$6 - 6 = 0$	No
$x = 7$	$7 - 6 = 1$	No
$x = 9$	$9 - 6 = 3$	No
$x = 11$	$11 - 6 = 5$	Yes

The solution to the equation is $x = 11$.

Solve each equation by testing these values for x: 1, 5, 6, 9.

1 $x - 1 = 8$ **2** $x + 7 = 13$ **3** $12 - x = 7$

4 $8 + x - 5 = 4$ **5** $x + 4 - 3 = 6$ **6** $15 - x = 9$

7 $2 + x = 7$ **8** $30 - x = 21$

Solve each equation by testing values for the variable.

9 $b + 6 = 18$ **10** $c - 4 = 2$ **11** $m + 8 = 9$

12 $y - 16 = 20$ **13** $22 - x = 20$ **14** $5 + n = 23$

15 $z - 7 = 12$ **16** $w + 13 = 17$ **17** $20 - k = 6$

Equations (continued)

Solve each equation by testing these values for x: 3, 7, 12, 18.

18 $x + 5 = 23$

_____

19 $17 - x = 10$

_____

20 $12 + x - 15 = 0$

_____

21 $20 - x = 2$

_____

22 $x - 6 = 6$

_____

23 $14 - x = 11$

_____

24 $10 + x = 28$

_____

25 $7 - x = 0$

_____

Solve each equation by testing values for the variable.

26 $s - 3 = 18$

_____

27 $w + 6 = 14$

_____

28 $t - 10 = 14$

_____

29 $n + 5 - 12 = 1$

_____

30 $32 - m = 5$

_____

31 $v + 7 = 20$

_____

32 **Math Reasoning** Does the equation $x - 6 = 8$ have the same solution as $x - 6 + 6 = 8 + 6$? Explain.

_____

_____

_____

33 **Test Prep** Choose the correct letter for each answer.

What is the solution to the equation $x - 9 = 11$?

A 20 **B** 18 **C** 2 **D** 11

34 Solve the equation $8 - x = 5$.

F 5 **G** 3 **H** 8 **J** 2

Equations

1 Which is the solution of $15 + x = 32$?

A 22

B 19

C 17

D 15

4 What is the solution of the equation $x + 18 = 25$?

F 7

G 8

H 9

J 10

2 What is the solution of the equation $19 - x = 15$?

F 14

G 15

H 9

J 4

5 Which of the following equations has $x = 16$ as a solution?

A $2 + x = 16$

B $21 - x = 5$

C $x + 4 = 12$

D $x - 16 = 8$

3 Which of the following equations has $x = 2$ as a solution?

A $x - 3 = 5$

B $x + 5 = 7$

C $2 - x = 3$

D $6 + x = 4$

6 Which is the solution of $7 - x = 0$?

F 9

G 8

H 7

J 0

Oral Directions Choose the correct letter for each answer.

Tell what you would do to find *n*. Then find *n*.

Rule:	
10	82
n	105
302	374

Name _____

Example 1

Tell what you would do to get the letter alone.

$$x - 37$$

$x - 37$ means 37 is subtracted from x.
Adding 37 gets x alone.
$x - 37 + 37 = x$

Example 2

For the table at the right, tell what you would do to find n.
Then find n.

To find n, add 35 to 50.
$n = 85$.

Rule: Subtract 35	
n	50
100	65
250	215

Tell what you would do to get the letter alone.

1 $x - 12$ **2** $n + 50$ **3** $23 + n$

_____ _____ _____

4 $w + 7$ **5** $x - 230$ **6** $435 + n$

_____ _____ _____

7 $213 + a$ **8** $m + 140$ **9** $z - 1$

_____ _____ _____

10 $10 + x$ **11** $n - 44$ **12** $w + 29$

_____ _____ _____

13 $m + 33$ **14** $47 + a$ **15** $z - 51$

_____ _____ _____

16 $n - 57$ **17** $x + 358$ **18** $47 + a$

_____ _____ _____

Name _____

Relating Addition and Subtraction (continued)

For each table, tell what you would do to find *n*. Then find *n*.

19

Rule: Subtract 61	
75	14
n	75
249	188

20

Rule: Add 74	
n	251
205	279
457	531

21

Rule: Subtract 90	
190	90
380	290
n	480

_____

_____

22

Rule: Add 15	
47	62
95	110
n	259

23

Rule: Subtract 55	
n	56
300	245
540	485

24

Rule: Add 700	
150	850
n	1,507
1,415	2,115

_____

_____

25 Max said, "I am thinking of a number. I get 23 if I add 14 to it." What is Max's number? _____

26 Antoinette said, "I am thinking of a number. I get 205 if I subtract 70 from it." What is Antoinette's number? _____

27 **Test Prep** Choose the correct letter for each answer.

Tell what you would do to get the letter alone.

   n − 47

A Subtract 47.   **C** Divide by 47.

B Multiply by 47.   **D** Add 47.

28 Find *n* for the table at the right.

F *n* = 453   **H** *n* = 365

G *n* = 443   **J** *n* = 375

Rule: Add 44	
n	409
488	532
679	723

Name _____

1 Tell what you would do to get the letter alone.

$$x - 79$$

A Add 79.

B Subtract 79.

C Multiply by 79.

D Divide by 79.

2 Tell what you would do to get the letter alone.

$$346 + n$$

F Add 346.

G Multiply by 346.

H Subtract 346.

J Divide by 346.

3 Omar said, "I am thinking of a number. If I subtract 65 from it, I get 59." What is Omar's number?

A 6

B 124

C 114

D 14

4 For the table below, find n.

Rule: Subtract 27	
54	27
n	221
320	293

F 106

G 194

H 204

J 248

5 For the table below, find n.

Rule: Add 83	
347	430
588	671
n	900

A 817

B 973

C 827

D 983

Oral Directions Choose the correct letter for each answer.

Robert's team needs 78 points to beat their old high score. They already have 49 points. How many more points must Robert's team score? Solve the equation $49 + m = 78$ to find the points needed.

Name _____

Solving Addition and Subtraction Equations

Example 1

Solve $x + 5 = 17$.

$$x + 5 = 17$$
$$x + 5 - 5 = 17 - 5$$
$$x = 12$$

Check: $x + 5 = 17$
$$12 + 5 = 17$$
$$17 = 17$$

> To get x by itself, subtract 5. To keep the sides equal, subtract 5 from both sides.

Example 2

Solve $n - 147 = 250$.

$$n - 147 = 250$$
$$n - 147 + 147 = 250 + 147$$
$$n = 397$$

Check: $n - 147 = 250$
$$397 - 147 = 250$$
$$250 = 250$$

> To get n by itself, add 147. To keep the sides equal, add 147 to both sides.

Solve each equation.

1 $w + 52 = 107$ _____

2 $n - 17 = 5$ _____

3 $77 = m + 8$ _____

4 $49 = a - 21$ _____

5 $y - 27 = 27$ _____

6 $0 = w - 10$ _____

7 $m + 414 = 520$ _____

8 $x - 74 = 100$ _____

9 $323 = a + 11$ _____

10 $122 = n - 147$ _____

11 $y + 54 = 98$ _____

12 $k - 407 = 515$ _____

13 $159 = n - 12$ _____

14 $a - 159 = 12$ _____

15 $205 = a + 148$ _____

16 $w + 376 = 981$ _____

17 $35 = x - 149$ _____

18 $y - 845 = 311$ _____

19 $178 = a + 167$ _____

20 $19 = n - 67$ _____

21 $m - 248 = 16$ _____

Solving Addition and Subtraction Equations (continued)

Solve each equation.

22 $376 = a - 467$

_____

23 $12 = x + 12$

_____

24 $47 = y - 385$

_____

25 $x - 446 = 203$

_____

26 $n - 210 = 307$

_____

27 $w + 432 = 433$

_____

28 $y - 211 = 365$

_____

29 $876 = a + 311$

_____

30 $216 = n - 4$

_____

31 $w + 654 = 1,000$

_____

32 $x - 852 = 900$

_____

33 $147 = n + 52$

_____

34 Ben started the day with $25.75. After a trip to the park and lunch, he had $8.17. Let n be the amount he spent. Write an equation to find n.

_____

35 A cold front moved in at noon and in 5 hours, the temperature had dropped 23°. The temperature at 5:00 P.M. was 14°. Let x be the temperature at noon. Write an equation to find x.

_____

36 Mental Math If 35 is added to a number to get 65, what was the number?

_____

37 Test Prep Choose the correct letter for each answer.

What is the solution of the equation $789 = n + 321$?

A $1,110 = n$ **B** $1,100 = n$ **C** $468 = n$ **D** $476 = n$

38 What is the solution of the equation $a - 128 = 128$?

F $a = 256$ **G** $a = 0$ **H** $a = 246$ **J** $a = 100$

Solving Addition and Subtraction Equations ADDITIONAL PRACTICE

1 What is the solution of the equation $n - 233 = 401$?

A $n = 168$

B $n = 262$

C $n = 634$

D $n = 272$

2 What is the solution to the equation $x + 64 = 212$?

F $x = 148$

G $x = 152$

H $x = 276$

J $x = 252$

3 What is the solution to the equation $311 = w - 19$?

A $292 = w$

B $308 = w$

C $330 = w$

D $208 = w$

4 Heide saved $64.12. She wants to buy a bike that costs $128.99. Let n be how much more she needs to save. Which equation below could be used to find n?

F $\$64.12 - n = \$128.99$

G $\$64.12 + n = \$128.99$

H $\$128.99 + \$64.12 = n$

J $n - \$64.12 = \$128.99$

5 A baseball team equipment manager had 785 baseballs in the stock room. He sent 128 baseballs with the team on a trip. Let w be the number of baseballs still in the stock room. Which equation below could be used to find w?

A $w + 785 = 128$

B $785 + 128 = w$

C $w - 128 = 785$

D $785 = w + 128$

Oral Directions Choose the correct letter for each answer.

© Scott Foresman

Jamie ate 5 peaches in one week and *b* peaches during another week. Write an expression for the total number of peaches Jamie ate in these two weeks.

Name _____

Example

Evaluate $3n$ when $n = 7$, $n = 25$, and $n = 255$.

When $n = 7$,	When $n = 25$,	When $n = 255$
$3n = 3 \times 7$	$3n = 3 \times 25$	$3n = 3 \times 255$
$= 21$	$= 75$	$= 765$

Evaluate each expression for $x = 16$, $x = 64$, and $x = 88$.

1 $x + 137$ **2** $\frac{x}{4}$ **3** $x - 9$ **4** $11x$

_____   _____   _____   _____

_____   _____   _____   _____

_____   _____   _____   _____

5 $411 + x$ **6** $\frac{x}{2}$ **7** $x + x$ **8** $10x$

_____   _____   _____   _____

_____   _____   _____   _____

_____   _____   _____   _____

Evaluate each expression for $x = 48$, $x = 54$, and $x = 96$.

9 $x - 12$ **10** $\frac{x}{6}$ **11** $8x$ **12** $x - 25$

_____   _____   _____   _____

_____   _____   _____   _____

_____   _____   _____   _____

13 $156 - x$ **14** $147 + x$ **15** $17x$ **16** $\frac{x}{2}$

_____   _____   _____   _____

_____   _____   _____   _____

Name _____

Using Expressions (continued)

Write each word phrase as an expression.

17 30 more than a number

_____

18 17 subtracted from a number

_____

19 a number divided by 8

_____

20 a number multiplied by 100

_____

21 a number increased by 51

_____

22 16 divided by a number

_____

23 44 multiplied by a number

_____

24 the sum of 63 and a number

_____

25 27 less than a number

_____

26 the product of a number and 72

_____

27 the product of 80 and a number

_____

28 93 less than a number

_____

29 Katrina is 8 years old. Write an expression for her age n years from now. _____

30 Three friends shared x cookies. Write an expression for the number of cookies each friend had. _____

31 **Math Reasoning** Write an expression for the number of feet in w miles. _____

32 **Test Prep** Choose the correct letter for the answer.

Evaluate the expression $n - 301$ for $n = 740$.

A 449　　　**B** 339　　　**C** 1,041　　　**D** 439

22

© Scott Foresman

Name _____

1 Evaluate the expression below for $n = 113$.

$$n + 430$$

A 973

B 543

C 327

D 317

4 Write the word phrase below as an expression.

317 less than a number

F $\frac{n}{317}$

G $317 - n$

H $n - 317$

J $317n$

2 Evaluate the expression below for $x = 295$.

$$332 - x$$

F 37

G 627

H 143

J 137

5 Write the word phrase below as an expression.

the product of 31 and a number

A $31 + n$

B $n - 31$

C $\frac{n}{31}$

D $31n$

3 Evaluate the expression below for $w = 996$.

$$\frac{w}{4}$$

A 3,984

B 249

C 992

D 1,000

6 Deborah is 4 years younger than her brother. Deborah is x years old. Find an expression for her brother's age.

F $x + 4$

G $x - 4$

H $4x$

J $4 - x$

Oral Directions Choose the correct letter for each answer.

The exact product of *n* and 40 is greater than 1,200. Is the product of *n* and 30 greater or less than 900?

Evaluating Expressions with Whole Numbers LESSON PRACTICE

Example

Evaluate $45 - 3n$ when $n = 2$, $n = 6$, and $n = 8$.

When $n = 2$,
$$45 - 3n = 45 - 3 \times 2$$
$$= 45 - 6$$
$$= 39$$

Replace n with 2.
Use the order of operations and multiply first.
Then add.

When $n = 6$,
$$45 - 3n = 45 - 3 \times 6$$
$$= 45 - 18$$
$$= 27$$

When $n = 8$,
$$45 - 3n = 45 - 3 \times 8$$
$$= 45 - 24$$
$$= 21$$

Evaluate each expression for $x = 6$ and $x = 9$.

1 $x + 1$ _____

2 $12 - x$ _____

3 $3x + 2$ _____

4 $5 + 2x$ _____

5 $24 - 2x$ _____

6 $2x - 7$ _____

7 $\dfrac{x}{3}$ _____

8 $4x - 3$ _____

9 $\dfrac{18}{x}$ _____

10 $x - 4$ _____

11 $7 + 4x$ _____

12 $\dfrac{x}{3} + 7$ _____

Evaluate each expression for $a = 8$ and $a = 12$.

13 $7a - 10$ _____

14 $16 + 3a$ _____

15 $\dfrac{a}{4}$ _____

16 $a + 4$ _____

17 $\dfrac{24}{a} + 1$ _____

18 $14 - a$ _____

19 $36 - 2a$ _____

20 $4a - 26$ _____

21 $5a$ _____

22 $\dfrac{48}{a} - 1$ _____

23 $15 - a$ _____

24 $4 + 4a$ _____

Evaluate each expression for $n = 3$ and $n = 9$.

25 $3n$ _____

26 $10 - n$ _____

27 $\dfrac{n}{3} + 4$ _____

Evaluating Expressions with Whole Numbers (continued)

Evaluate each expression for $b = 2$ and $b = 0$.

28 $2b + 3$ _____ **29** $\dfrac{b}{2}$ _____ **30** $14 - 3b$ _____

31 $7 - \dfrac{b}{2}$ _____ **32** $5b$ _____ **33** $14 + 5b$ _____

Evaluate each expression for $x = 6$ and $x = 12$.

34 $4x$ _____ **35** $\dfrac{x}{2} + 6$ _____ **36** $8 + 6x$ _____

37 $40 - x$ _____ **38** $2x - 3$ _____ **39** $7x - 1$ _____

40 Evaluate the expressions $5(w + 2)$ and $5w + 10$ for $w = 4$.

_____

_____

41 **Math Reasoning** What do you notice about your answers in Exercise 40? Will this happen when w is any whole number? Explain.

_____

_____

42 **Test Prep** Choose the correct letter for each answer.

Evaluate the expression $24 - 3n$ for $n = 8$.

A 8   **B** 0   **C** 16   **D** 48

43 Evaluate the expression $\dfrac{a}{3} - 2$ for $a = 30$.

F 8   **G** 10   **H** 25   **J** 12

Name _____

Evaluating Expressions with Whole Numbers ADDITIONAL PRACTICE

1 Evaluate the expression for $n = 15$.

$$15 + 3n$$

A 270

B 90

C 45

D 60

2 Evaluate the expression for $w = 7$.

$$26 - 2w$$

F 168

G 12

H 17

J 15

3 Evaluate the expression for $x = 12$.

$$12x$$

A 144

B 24

C 36

D 48

4 Evaluate the expression for $a = 0$.

$$4a + 6$$

F 10

G 6

H 46

J 20

5 Evaluate the expression for $n = 10$.

$$23 + \frac{n}{5}$$

A 2

B 21

C 25

D 27

6 Evaluate the expression for $w = 2$.

$$\frac{24}{w} - 5$$

F 7

G 43

H 12

J 9

Oral Directions Choose the correct letter for each answer.

© Scott Foresman

Tell what you would do to find *n*. Then find *n*.

Rule:	
3	90
9	270
15	*n*

Name _____

Example

Tell what you would do to get the letter alone:

$n \times 12$

You would divide by 12 because division can undo multiplication.

....

Tell what you would do to get each letter alone.

1 $a \times 5$

_____

_____

2 $\dfrac{m}{15}$

_____

_____

3 $x \div 25$

_____

_____

4 $16b$

_____

_____

5 $y \times 30$

_____

_____

6 $\dfrac{z}{24}$

_____

_____

7 $65n$

_____

_____

8 $\dfrac{c}{27}$

_____

_____

9 $\dfrac{t}{95}$

_____

_____

10 $45r$

_____

_____

11 $s \div 17$

_____

_____

12 $\dfrac{v}{72}$

_____

_____

13 $\dfrac{y}{62}$

_____

_____

14 $z \div 43$

_____

_____

15 $37x$

_____

_____

Relating Multiplication and Division (continued)

Tell what you would do to get each letter alone.

16 $n \times 25$

_____

_____

17 $\frac{m}{64}$

_____

_____

18 $81x$

_____

_____

19 $15r$

_____

_____

20 $t \div 56$

_____

_____

21 $\frac{L}{72}$

_____

_____

For each table, tell what you would do to get n alone. Then find n.

22

Rule: Multiply by 5	
10	50
15	75
n	200

23

Rule: Divide by 30	
90	3
210	7
n	12

_____

_____

24 Make a table that has the rule "Multiply by 12." Complete the table when the values in the second column are 72, 108, and 144.

25 **Mental Math** If you multiply a certain number by 2, the answer is 24. What is the number? _____

26 **Test Prep** Choose the correct letter for the answer.

What would you do to get the letter alone? $12x$

A Multiply by 12.   **C** Multiply by x.

B Divide by 12.   **D** Divide by x.

Name _____

Relating Multiplication and Division

1 Tell what you would do to get *n* alone.

$$12n$$

A Multiply by 12.

B Divide by 12.

C Multiply by *n*.

D Divide by *n*.

2 Tell what you would do to get *x* alone.

$$\frac{x}{35}$$

F Multiply by 35.

G Divide by 35.

H Multiply by *x*.

J Divide by *x*.

3 What is the missing number in Column A?

A 13

B 14

C 15

D 17

A	B
2	10
7	35
■	75
17	85
23	115
32	■

4 Tell what you would do to get *b* alone.

$$b \times 16$$

F Multiply by 16.

G Divide by 16.

H Multiply by *b*.

J Divide by *b*.

Use the table below for Exercises 5 and 6.

A	B
3	9
6	18
9	27
12	36
15	●
●	54

5 What is the missing number in Column A?

A 9   C 28

B 18   D 48

6 What is the missing number in Column B?

F 5   H 45

G 21   J 60

Oral Directions Choose the correct letter for each answer.

© Scott Foresman

Matt uses plastic sleeves to organize his baseball cards. Each sleeve holds 8 cards. He fills 12 sleeves. How many baseball cards does he have? If c is the number of cards, use $\frac{c}{8} = 12$ to find c.

Solving Multiplication and Division Equations LESSON PRACTICE

Example

Solve the equation:

$9n = 72$

Because division can undo multiplication, you would divide both sides by 9.

$n = 8$

Solve each equation.

1 $4a = 16$

_____

2 $\frac{m}{15} = 2$

_____

3 $7x = 56$

_____

4 $16b = 32$

_____

5 $10y = 40$

_____

6 $\frac{z}{24} = 3$

_____

7 $15n = 90$

_____

8 $\frac{c}{12} = 7$

_____

9 $\frac{t}{9} = 20$

_____

10 $19r = 38$

_____

11 $35s = 140$

_____

12 $\frac{v}{72} = 4$

_____

13 $6m = 54$

_____

14 $\frac{a}{13} = 4$

_____

15 $21d = 105$

_____

Solving Multiplication and Division Equations (continued)

Solve each equation.

16 $20n = 200$

_____

17 $\frac{m}{64} = 4$

_____

18 $8x = 48$

_____

19 $15r = 120$

_____

20 $\frac{t}{16} = 5$

_____

21 $\frac{l}{7} = 14$

_____

22 There are 5 rows of desks in a classroom and each row has the same number of desks. There are 35 desks altogether. If d represents the number of desks in each row, circle the equation below that can be used to find d.

$35d = 5$ $5d = 35$ $\frac{d}{35} = 5$ $\frac{d}{5} = 35$

23 **Math Reasoning** Write and solve an equation: A number divided by 6 equals 15.

_____

24 **Test Prep** Choose the correct letter for each answer.

Solve $3x = 36$.

A $x = 10$ **B** $x = 108$ **C** $x = 12$ **D** $x = 21$

25 Solve $\frac{n}{7} = 15$.

F $n = 2$ **G** $n = 105$ **H** $n = \frac{1}{2}$ **J** $n = 20$

Name _____

1 Solve for n.
$$3n = 42$$

A $n = 14$

B $n = 126$

C $n = \frac{14}{3}$

D $n = 45$

2 Solve for x.
$$\frac{x}{7} = 35$$

F $x = 5$

G $x = 245$

H $x = 42$

J $x = \frac{7}{35}$

3 There are 4 quarters in each dollar. Rayna has 48 quarters. If d is the number of dollars that Rayna has, which equation below can be used to find d?

A $4d = 48$

B $48d = 4$

C $4d = 12$

D $\frac{d}{4} = 48$

4 Three friends shared some marbles equally among themselves. Each person received 9 marbles. If m is the total number of marbles, which equation can be used to find m?

F $3m = 9$

G $\frac{m}{3} = 9$

H $9m = 3$

J $\frac{m}{9} = 27$

5 Solve for a.
$$12a = 24$$

A $a = 288$

B $a = \frac{1}{2}$

C $a = 0.5$

D $a = 2$

6 Solve for w.
$$\frac{w}{30} = 6$$

F $w = 5$

G $w = 180$

H $w = 30$

J $w = 36$

Oral Directions Choose the correct letter for each answer.

Lucy plans to save $5.25 every month. Write an expression for her savings rate for m months of savings. Then find her savings for 3, 6, 9, and 12 months.

Name _____

Example

Evaluate the expression for $x = 0.03$ and $x = 2.3$.

$2x + 1$

$2(0.03) + 1$ $2(2.3) + 1$

$= 0.06 + 1$ $= 4.6 + 1$

$= 1.06$ $= 5.6$

Evaluate each expression for $x = 0.05$, $x = 0.14$, and $x = 3.2$.

1 $3x$

_____

2 $x + 5$

_____

3 $2.1 + x$

_____

4 $7.3 - x$

_____

5 $13.24 + x$

_____

6 $2.1x$

_____

7 $3x + 1.5$

_____

8 $25x - 1.1$

_____

9 $8.3 - 2x$

_____

10 $x + 3.7$

_____

11 $6x + 4$

_____

12 $5.4x$

_____

Evaluating Expressions with Decimals (continued)

Evaluate each expression for $x = 0.07$, $x = 0.21$, and $x = 8.2$.

13 $x + 3.7$

_____

14 $15 - x$

_____

15 $4.7x$

_____

16 $2x + 5.6$

_____

17 $4.1x - 0.1$

_____

18 $3.5 + 7x$

_____

19 Ryan bought some boxes of cereal and spent $9.45. Write an expression for the price spent for b boxes. Then find the price per box if he bought 5 boxes. _____

20 **Math Reasoning** Jason earned $204 last week and he worked 30 hours. If he was paid the same rate per hour this week and works 40 hours, how much will he earn? _____

21 **Test Prep** Choose the correct letter for the answer.

Evaluate the expression for $x = 5.7$.

$3.2x - 7.97$

A 11.97   **B** 13.67   **C** 10.27   **D** 21.66

Name _____

1 Evaluate the expression $3x$ for $x = 1.7$

A 51

B 5.1

C 2.0

D 1.4

2 Evaluate the expression $x + 4.5$ for $x = 7.8$.

F 3.3

G 12.3

H 1.23

J 35.1

3 Alex earned $30.50 yesterday. Find the expression for his hourly rate for h hours of work.

A $\dfrac{\$30.50}{h}$

B $\dfrac{h}{\$30.50}$

C $\$30.50h$

D $\$30.50 + h$

4 Kim bought a 12.5-ounce package of crackers. Find the expression for the number of calories, c, per ounce.

F 12.5c

G $\dfrac{c}{12.5}$

H 12.5/c

J $c + 12.5$

5 Evaluate the expression $x - 0.9$ for $x = 1.1$.

A 2.0

B 0.99

C 0.2

D 0.02

6 Evaluate the expression $2x + 3.2$ for $x = 8.3$.

F 19.8

G 23

H 16.6

J 14.7

Oral Directions Choose the correct letter for each answer.

© Scott Foresman

Marie found a pair of pants on sale for $\frac{1}{4}$ off the original price. If the pants are regularly priced at $28, how much money will she save during the sale? Use the expression $\frac{1}{4}p$, where p is the original price.

Name _____

Evaluating Expressions with Fractions

LESSON PRACTICE

Example 1

Evaluate $3\frac{3}{4} - n$, when $n = 2\frac{1}{8}$.

$3\frac{3}{4} - n = 3\frac{3}{4} - 2\frac{1}{8} = 3\frac{6}{8} - 2\frac{1}{8} = 1\frac{5}{8}$

Example 2

Tennis rackets are on sale for $\frac{1}{4}$ off the original price. Use the expression $\frac{1}{4}p$ to find the savings on a tennis racket that originally cost $64.

Evaluate $\frac{1}{4}p$ when $p = \$64$.

$\frac{1}{4}p = \frac{1}{4} \times 64 = \frac{1}{4} \times \frac{64}{1} = \frac{64}{4} = 16$

The savings on the tennis racket is $16.

· ·

Evaluate.

1 $5\frac{1}{3} - m$, when $m = 3\frac{1}{6}$

_____

2 $\frac{2}{3}x$, when $x = \frac{3}{4}$

_____

3 $n \div 4$, when $n = \frac{5}{6}$

_____

4 $\frac{1}{5} \div y$, when $y = \frac{3}{4}$

_____

5 $d + 1\frac{4}{5}$, when $d = 2\frac{1}{10}$

_____

6 $r - \frac{5}{8}$, when $r = 1\frac{3}{8}$

_____

7 $\frac{2}{5} - c$, when $c = \frac{3}{10}$

_____

8 $\frac{1}{5}b$, when $b = \frac{2}{5}$

_____

© Scott Foresman

41

Name _____

Evaluating Expressions with Fractions (continued)

Evaluate $\frac{5}{6} + k$, when $k =$

9 $\frac{1}{12}$ _____   **10** $\frac{1}{4}$ _____   **11**   3 _____

Evaluate $t - 1\frac{1}{4}$, when $t =$

12 $3\frac{1}{12}$ _____   **13**   5 _____   **14** $2\frac{3}{4}$ _____

Evaluate $\frac{1}{8} x$, when $x =$

15   24 _____   **16** $\frac{2}{3}$ _____   **17** $4\frac{2}{5}$ _____

18   A CD is on sale for $\frac{1}{3}$ off the original price. Use $\frac{1}{3} p$
to find the savings on a CD that originally cost $15. _____

19   What is the price for a CD on sale for $\frac{1}{4}$ off the original
price that originally cost $12? _____

20   **Math Reasoning** If you received $\frac{1}{3}$ off the original
price, what fraction of the original price would you pay? _____

21   **Test Prep** Choose the correct letter for each answer.

Evaluate $m - 1\frac{2}{5}$, when $m = 2\frac{1}{10}$.

A $\frac{7}{10}$ **B** $1\frac{1}{5}$ **C** $1\frac{1}{10}$ **D** $1\frac{3}{10}$

22   Athletic shoes are on sale for $\frac{1}{4}$ off the original price. Use $\frac{1}{4} p$
to find the savings on athletic shoes that cost $72.

F $4   **G** $6   **H** $18   **J** $288

Evaluating Expressions with Fractions

1 Evaluate $m \div 5$, when $m = \frac{2}{3}$.

A $3\frac{1}{3}$

B $\frac{2}{15}$

C $\frac{3}{10}$

D $7\frac{1}{2}$

2 A sale offers $\frac{2}{3}$ off the original price of T-shirts. If a T-shirt originally cost \$15, what is the amount of savings?

F \$2

G \$3

H \$5

J \$10

3 Evaluate $s - \frac{1}{8}$, when $s = 2\frac{3}{16}$.

A 2

B $2\frac{1}{4}$

C $2\frac{1}{16}$

D $2\frac{1}{8}$

4 Which of the following shows $\frac{2}{3}p$ when $p = 36$?

F 12

G 14

H 54

J 24

5 Find $1\frac{3}{4} + n$, when $n = 2\frac{1}{8}$.

A $1\frac{5}{8}$

B $3\frac{5}{8}$

C $3\frac{7}{8}$

D 4

6 A pair of jeans is on sale for $\frac{1}{4}$ off the original price. If the jeans originally cost \$48, what is the sale price?

F \$36

G \$40

H \$42

J \$46

Oral Directions Choose the correct letter for each answer.

Tools Contents

10 × 10 Chart

Name _____

Word Web